CW00386404

Explaining Principalities and Powers

Tom Marshall

Sovereign World

Scripture quotations, unless otherwise indicated,
are taken from the NIV The Holy Bible, New International Version.
© Copyright 1973, 1978, New York International Bible Society.
Published by Hodder & Stoughton.

RSV, Revised Standard Version.
© Copyright 1946, 1952 by the Division of Christian Education
of the National Council of the Churches of Christ
in the United States of America.

ASB, American Standard Version of the Bible.
© Copyright The Lockman Foundation 1960, 1962, 1963, 1968, 1975, 1977,
La Habra, California.

ISBN: 1 85240 087 0

SOVEREIGN WORLD LIMITED
P.O. Box 777, Tonbridge, Kent TN11 9XT, England.

Contents

Contents

Introduction

As Christians we are continually aware that we live in a fallen world that is unfavourable to the Gospel and often actively antagonistic to it.

In the secular spheres of society, in the realms of business, commerce, politics and entertainment, we are conscious of a self confident ruthlessness and a hedonistic godlessness that often intimidate us. On Sunday in church we may sing the victorious hymns of Zion and militant songs about "taking the land", but if we are honest we will admit that in the workplace on Monday morning most of us feel almost totally helpless.

In Ephesians 6:12 Paul identifies the locus of the conflict as follows:

> *"For our struggle is not against flesh and blood, but against the rulers, against the authorities, against the powers of this dark world and against the spiritual forces of evil in the heavenly realms."*

If we are to be the overcomers we are meant to be, we need to know the true characteristics of the conflict we face, the nature of the "land" we are meant to take, and the real identity of the enemies that oppose us.

More importantly, we must understand that the source of our victory, is the death of Jesus Christ on the Cross and his resurrection from the dead, or what the Bible calls the blood of the Lamb (Revelation 12:11). But to face the powers with confidence we must really know how and why the Cross has such awesome power. These are the topics that we will address in the pages that follow.

1

An Overview of the Battlefield

We have, as it were, arrived on this earthly scene to find ourselves in the middle of a spiritual battle, one moreover in which there are no exempt civilians and no neutral territories. Therefore we need to be clear first of all as to what is going on and why, and second, what our place is in the conflict.

The Bible reveals the existence of a cosmic conflict between God and Satan in which the battlefield is this earth and the human race. *At issue is Satan's attempt to separate God from his creation word, that is, his declared intent and purpose to have:*

1. Man in his image, after his likeness and having dominion (Genesis 1:28);

2. The whole earth filled with his glory (Numbers 14:21; Habakkuk 2:14);

3. All things in heaven and on earth together under the headship of Christ (Ephesians 1:10).

To get the right perspective on the form that this struggle has taken we need to go back to the beginnings, that is to creation and the fall.

Creation

All creation, Paul tells us, is Christ centred, he is its source, its architect and its end.

"For by Him were all things created, both in the heavens and on earth, visible and invisible, whether thrones or dominions or rulers or authorities – all things have been created by Him and for Him. And He is before all things, and in Him all things hold together." (Colossians 1:16-17, ASB)

"For from him and through him and to him are all things."
(Romans 11:36)

When we ask, "What is outside the 'all things' of creation?", the answer is, "nothing". When we ask "What is included in the 'all things' of creation?", we can distinguish the following three important categories:

1. *Reality structured in two dimensions or realms.*
a. The Spiritual realm and within it the angelic/demonic orders.
b. The material realm and within it the orders of nature.

2. *Mankind inhabiting both the material and the spiritual realm.*

3. *The things that mankind has created,* that is; cultures, societies, organisations, institutions, constructions, technologies, sciences, art etc.

The Creation Mandate
The biblical destiny of mankind is set out in what is called the creation mandate, sometimes the dominion mandate or the cultural mandate. It is the charge God gave to mankind to steward the created earth and unfold its meaning.

"God blessed them and said to them, 'Be fruitful and increase in number; fill the earth and subdue it. Rule over the fish of the sea and the birds of the air and over every living creature that moves on the ground.'" (Genesis 1:28)

The creation mandate had two enabling commands, (1) Be fruitful and increase, and (2) Rule over the earth.

The Family
The first of these commands began to be fulfilled with the beginning of the human family (Genesis 4:1). The importance of the family, and the reason for the constant satanic pressure and attack on the family lies in the fact that it is a divinely ordained institution that has to do with man's destiny in relation to the earth.

The City
The second enabling command began to be fulfilled in the building of the first city.

> *"Cain lay with his wife, and she became pregnant and gave birth to Enoch. Cain was then building a city, and he named it after his son Enoch."* (Genesis 4:17)

Henceforth all Bible history centres around cities. The names of some are household words when we think of biblical topics – Babylon and Nineveh, Tyre and Sidon, Sodom and Gomorrah, Rome and Jerusalem, Damascus, Samaria, Jericho, Antioch, Athens and Caesarea Philippi. There are also dozens of others whose names are unfamiliar and strange and whose significance we no longer understand.

It is to the inner history of the city that we have to turn in the next chapter but we need to understand its importance to the whole of our present study. Note the following points to which we will return in more detail later.

1. The city is the enduring symbol throughout Scripture for what man corporately creates. Thus:

a. *At the macro level* it stands in political terms for the state or the nation, and in sociological terms for the entire culture of a nation or people. The first states were city states and the major empires of antiquity. For example the Babylonian, Assyrian and Roman were founded on cities; when the city fell, the empire fell.

b. *At the micro level* the city also stands as a symbol for all the individual structures within a state or society. For example, a business corporation, a school, a town council, a club, or even a local church, are in every sense of the word, little "cities".

2. *The symbol of the city in the Old Testament stands for the same realities that are termed in the New Testament the "principalities and powers",* in all their various manifestations – thrones, dominions, rulers and authorities. These are all recognisable in our modern society in exactly the same operations.

a. *Thrones* are the symbolic ways of expressing the authority invested in an office that is continuous over time regardless of its current occupant. We speak of the "bench", for the authority of the law court judges, the "chair" for the one presiding at a meeting, the "oval office" for the presidency of the United States or "No. 10 Downing Street" for the office of Prime Minister in Britain. They are all thrones.

b. *Dominions* are the spheres of influence over which thrones preside or hold sway. It may be visible, the territory of a State government, or the city limits for example, or invisible as when we speak of "the power of the press."

c. *Rulers* are the incumbents holding the office, that is, the investiture of power in a person. It is therefore not the person as such, but the person-in-office; for example, not just John Brown but Mayor John Brown is a ruler.

d. *Authorities* are the legitimations and sanctions by which authority is maintained, such as laws, regulations, rules, codes and constitutions, both written and customary.

The Fall

In the Fall, not only does mankind sin, but the dominion mandate turns against God.

10

1. *Man builds his cities as the expression of his destiny to rule, but he does it in rebellion.* Thus the city Babel, becomes the expression of man's corporate rebellion against God, a rebellion so ominous that it brought divine intervention (Genesis 11:1-9).

2. *In the Fall, man loses his spiritual authority over creation and into the power vacuum thus created, Satan comes and* establishes his demonic principalities and powers in the heavenly realm. These powers likewise appear in association with the city in the Old Testament. The Hebrew word for city also means "The Watching Angel", thus behind the structural power of the city we find the watching angel, the demon god of the city. The Bible names many of them – Baal, Dagon, Timmutz, Moloch, Ashtoreth, Chemosh, Adrammalech, Diana, Rimmon, Nergal and others.

Rebellion

In the Fall, God therefore faces rebellion against his will at three levels:

a. Level I The individual rebellion of fallen men and women.

b. Level II The corporate rebellion of the city, the fallen structures, and

c. Level III The satanic rebellion of the demonic powers.

Level I is the realm of flesh and blood. Levels II and III are the realm of spirit, and it is essential we distinguish them, both from Level I and from each other.
Turn again to Ephesians 6:12 where it is clearly expressed.

"For our struggle is not against flesh and blood... (Level I)

but against the rulers, against the authorities, against the powers of this dark world... (Level II)

11

and against the spiritual forces of evil in the heavenly realms." ...
(Level III)

The importance of this understanding will emerge as we go on.

2

The City, and the
Structural Powers

In the Old Testament, almost as soon as the city appears it
becomes a major factor in human history. Civilisation, culture,
learning, and technology flourish in the city. It becomes the
magnet for wealth, economic power, political influence and
colonisation, but it also becomes the focus of military power,
conquest, slavery and oppression and the centre of idolatry and
the occult. It is important to see why and how this is so because
we now live in the age of the mega city and the super power. It
has been estimated that by the year 2000 almost 70% of the
world's population will live in cities. The city has grown to
gigantic stature.

The city is named.

From its beginning with Cain the city is always named. In the Bible,
names always express character or identity, therefore the city once
named also acquires a distinctive character. Thus Nineveh is *"the
mistress of sorceries"* (Nahum 3:4), Tyre is *"the city of revelry,"*
(Isaiah 23:7), Babylon *"the mother of harlots"* (Revelation 17:5),
and Damascus *"the city of renown"* (Jeremiah 49:25).

It is the same today. London has a character that distinguishes
it from Paris or Sydney, Berne is different from Seoul, New York
is unlike Chicago and so on. Even a corporation or a church has
its own individual culture or character that is immediately noticed
by newcomers.

The city becomes a power.

This is a very important concept to grasp. A city (or a company or an institution), is created by, and lives through the corporate decisions of men and women, each of whom has a human spirit. When this corporate entity begins to function as such, there eventually comes into being a corporate spirit that embodies the character or personality of the organisation and gives it its individuality and distinctiveness. This corporate spirit or persona becomes a created reality in its own right. It is distinct from the people who at any time make up the inhabitants or members of the city. For example, what is London? It is not the people who now live in London, because 100 years ago none of them were born but London was there. In 100 years time none of the present inhabitants of London will be alive, but London will be alive and well.

Although it calls it "a legal fiction" the legal system recognises something like this when it treats a registered company as a separate entity from the shareholders who own it. The company can sue its own shareholders and in turn be sued by them, and even if all the shareholders die the company remains in existence.

Here are some of the features of this corporate spirit or personality of the city.

1. Although it is created by its founders, the city becomes increasingly independent of them. Instead of being shaped by people, it shapes them; it develops its own inner culture and ways of functioning to which people have to conform. This is true of a business corporation, a college, a government department, a football club, or a church. In the case of a church it is this corporate spirit or personality that in the letters to the seven churches in the book of Revelation is called the "angel" of the church (Revelation 1:20; 2:1, 8, 12, 18; 3:1, 7, 14).

2. Although its character is originally malleable and able to be shaped, the corporate spirit of the city becomes increasingly set in its ways and resistant to change. Thus characteristically an established church always resists renewal, and a culture never changes without upheaval and trauma.

3. Originally created to serve the people, the city ends up using the people to serve its own ends. Whether in the form of a corporation or a service club or a church, the "it" demands loyalty, and commitment and obedience, and rewards those who serve it well.

4. Its predominant instinct is for survival. Babylon, the city says to itself, *"I will continue for ever – the eternal queen!... I will never be a widow or suffer the loss of children."* (Isaiah 47:7, 8). People live and die, the city endures, staff come and go, the corporation goes on in perpetuity. Under threat it will use any means to survive and pay any price to maintain itself in existence.

The city is fallen

Because the "it" is created by fallen men, the city is also fallen, and, with Babel, becomes the expression of man's corporate rebellion against God (Genesis 11:1-9). But note the following important points:

1. The city in itself is not demonic, but it is fallen, that is to say it does some good things but also some evil things, it has legitimate ends but also strives for sinful and illegitimate ends.

2. One mark of the city's fallenness is its drive to become idolatrous, in other words it strives to be the ultimate value in people's lives and claims ultimate authority over them. It wants its interests to come before family, before personal interests, before health, before God.

God says,

> *"I am God, and there is no other; I am God, and there is none like me."* (Isaiah 46:9)

Babylon says,

> *"I am, and there is none besides me."* (Isaiah 47:8)

15

Tyre says,

> *"I am a god; I sit on the throne of a god."* (Ezekiel 28:2)

3. Idolatry however, inevitably leads to demonisation. In discussing food offered to idols, Paul points out that the idols are nothing, but behind the idols there are demons receiving the worship (1 Corinthians 10:10-20). Thus, a corporate structure can be demonised in the same way as an individual.

4. Nevertheless, the city, even in its fallenness is not to be rejected and not to be abandoned. Firstly because it is the object of redemption, and secondly because restored and transformed, it is required for the service of God in the age to come.

The Character of the City

The character of the fallen, rebellious city is analysed with great accuracy and insight in Scripture. It is essential for us to understand it so that we know what we are up against in living in the city, and all its manifestations great and small.

We are not dealing here with flesh and blood, that is with the sins of people (Ephesians 6:12), but with the dimension of structural evil that works through people, fostering rampant greed, capitalising on lust, inflaming violence and ruthlessly exploiting the weak and the helpless.

1. Because of its idolatrous drive, the city is not merely secular, and therefore religiously neutral, it is against God.

a. It blasphemes God (Isaiah 37:23-4), defies him (Jeremiah 50:29), and plots evil against him (Nahum 1:11).

b. It is full of idols, sorcery and witchcraft (Isaiah 47:9, Jeremiah 50:30; Nahum 3:4; Revelation 18:23).

c. It is against the church, the Lord's inheritance (Jeremiah 50:11).

16

2. *Its chief aim is self-aggrandisement* and it will use anything, including the Gospel and the Name of Christ to build up its status and position (Isaiah 13:10; 47:5; Jeremiah 51:41).

The drive of the city for greatness is manifested in:

a. The accumulation of wealth (Ezekiel 28:4-5; Revelation 18:14-15).

b. Architectural splendour and impressive constructions (Ezekiel 27; 3-12; Zechariah 9:3).

c. A consumption economy, majoring on luxury and entertainment (Isaiah 23:7; Ezekiel 26:17; Revelation 18:3, 7).

d. Self-confidence and an illusion of security (Zephaniah 2:15; Isaiah 47:8; Obadiah 3).

e. Economic power, often based on dishonest trading, and exploitation of men and women (Isaiah 23:3-9; Amos 1:9; Ezekiel 27:12-23; 28:16-18).

f. Expansion, conquest and colonisation, seen in modern times in takeovers and multinational conglomorates (Isaiah 14:21; Jeremiah 50:23; Ezekiel 26:17).

g. Wisdom and understanding put to corrupt purposes (Isaiah 47:10; Ezekiel 28:17).

3. *The fallenness of the city further manifested in its characteristic forms of evil that include:*

a. Violence and cruelty (Nahum 3:1-3; Ezekiel 28:160).

b. Arrogance and pride (Isaiah 10:12; Zechariah 10:11).

c. Ruthlessness and aggression (Isaiah 14:4-6; Ezekiel 30:11; 32:12).

d. Merciless oppression (Isaiah 14:17; 47:6).

e. dishonesty and injustice (Ezekiel 9:9; Nahum 3:1).

f. Wickedness, evil standards (Jonah 1:1; Nahum 1:11; Isaiah 47:10).

g. It destroys, devours and creates emptiness (Jeremiah 51:25, 35).

Understanding the Structural Powers

An understanding of the corporate spirit or personality helps to clarify some of the situations we commonly experience in the city. Here are some examples:

1. The sometimes rigid, implacable and irrational resistance to change in an organisation of otherwise adaptable, reasonable and progressive individuals.

What we have come up against is the spirit of the organisation that once set in its ways, is highly resistant to change.

2. The bitter power struggle that often takes place at an impalpable and suprahuman level in a business takeover, and why certain members of the management team of the business that has been captured are rapidly and ruthlessly dumped.

There is a life and death struggle between two cities and to the city, survival takes precedence over ethics, and the end will always justify the means. When one city wins, the people in the conquered city who are dropped, are not fired because of inefficiency but because they are not acceptable to, or don't "fit", the persona or spirit of the victorious city.

3. Why a church split is so devastating and so painful and leaves people hurt and scarred. The corporate spirit, the "angel" of the church has been wounded and amputated.

4. Why a breakaway group formed by disgruntled, divisive people often becomes a bitter, divided church. The persona that is created has the difficult characteristics of the founding flock.

5. Why the pervasiveness and seeming omnipotence of the city creates a feeling of helplessness amongst Christians and fosters a retreat from the secular city into the Christian "safe houses", that are the churches.

The skyline of the downtown area of the city is dominated by towering office blocks. They are the "high places". The gleaming skyscrapers are making a spiritual statement, "Here, we have the power! Here, we have the influence! Here, we command the resources! Here, you bow the knee to us!"

3

The Enemy in the Heavenlies

Under the dominion mandate, mankind had been given spiritual authority over the created world, that is:

1. They were to represent the source of power in the world, that is God.

2. They were to exercise the prerogatives of that power over creation in order to see that God's will was done on earth as it is in heaven, and

3. They were stewards, that is accountable to God for the way in which they fulfilled their role.

Because of the Fall, however, mankind lost access to the presence of God, therefore his authority over the world collapsed because it was no longer backed up by God's power. Into the spiritual vacuum that resulted, *Satan came and usurped the place of authority. Now, opposed to the kingdom of God, there is a dominion of darkness (Colossians 1:13), a ruling system of demonic "powers" that dominate the structural "powers" of the world system and harden them in their rebellion against God.*

If they are left to work unhindered these demonic powers will:

a. Bring confusion and chaos into attempts to diagnose the real nature of the problems in society or to discover viable solutions to the problems.

b. Seek to neutralise any potential threats to their control by spiritual or other attacks against anyone who represents a danger to that control, and

c. Frustrate attempts to reform the structural powers by hardening their resistance to change.

When we examine the nature of this domain of darkness we find a tightly knit hierarchy of evil powers. Here is a brief summary of the biblical evidence.

Satan

The dominion of darkness is under the direction and control of Satan, the fallen archangel. Two main passages describe his state and his fall (Isaiah 14:12-14, and Ezekiel 28:12-17).

1. In his unfallen state he was Lucifer, the morning star, son of the dawn. His realm was in heaven (Isaiah 14:12) and the Garden of Eden (Ezekiel 28:13).

2. Created blameless, he was the model of perfection, wisdom and beauty. He was a guardian cherub, that is with a particular role to do with the throne of God (Ezekiel 28:12-15).

3. Pride corrupted his wisdom (Ezekiel 28:17) and he aspired to the very throne of God, that is, to be equal with God.

> "I will raise my throne above the stars (angels) of God; I will sit enthroned on the mount of assembly, on the utmost heights of the sacred mountain. I will ascend above the tops of the clouds; I will make myself like the Most High."
>
> (Isaiah 14:13-14)

4. In his unfallen state Satan was anointed, that is he had the Holy Spirit. *When he sinned therefore, he sinned against the anointing, that is, his sin was the unpardonable sin against the Holy Spirit* (Matthew 3:29).

22

5. Because of his rebellion he was expelled in disgrace (Ekeziel 28:16) and cast down to earth (Isaiah 14:12; Luke 10:18).

6. Now Satan is Beelzebul (*"Baal is prince"*) the prince or ruler (archon) of the demons (Matthew 12:24). He is also called the prince of this world (John 12:31; 14:30), and the god of this age (2 Corinthians 4:4). Moreover he is the *"prince of the power of the air, the spirit that is now at work in the sons of disobedience"* (Ephesians 2:2 RSV). Here the meaning is that he controls the spiritual atmosphere or climate of the fallen world.

7. As far as the Church is concerned, Satan is the enemy (1 Peter 5:8), the accuser or devil (Revelation 12:10; Ephesians 4:27), the deceiver and father of lies (2 Corinthians 11:13-14; John 8:44), and the tempter (1 Thessalonians 3:5).

8. His character is revealed in his names. Thus he is *"the evil one"* (Matthew 13:38; Ephesians 6:16; 1 John 5:19), Apollyon, *"the destroyer"* (Revelation 9:11), Belial, the spirit of worthlessness and emptiness (2 Corinthians 6:15), and murderer (John 8:44). The animal images used to describe him are those of serpent (Genesis 3:1ff; 2 Corinthians 11:3), dragon (Revelation 12:9; 13:2; 20:2), and prowling lion (1 Peter 5:8).

9. Finally Satan's resources are described as including a throne or seat of power (Revelation 2:13; 16:10), strongholds (2 Corinthians 10:4), and secret ways of working (deep things), including the power to perform counterfeit miracles and signs (2 Thessalonians 2:7-9; Revelation 2:24).

A Host of Fallen Angels

Satan is neither omnipotent, nor is he omnipresent, therefore he works through a host of fallen angels, perhaps one third of the heavenly hosts, who followed him in his rebellion (Revelation 1:24; 2 Peter 2:4). These beings are also called demons (Matthew 9:33-4; Luke 8:27ff) and evil spirits or unclean spirits (Luke 8:29; Mark 9:25).

This army of evil spirit beings, organised in a hierarchy of demonic power structures dependent on the power of Satan, hold sway over the world system. They influence, manipulate and control the structural powers, confirming them in their rebellion against God, and using them as instruments of evil and oppression.

The shape of this structure is as follows:

1. Geopolitical and geographic, or territorial powers

a. World rulers (kosmoskrator) Ephesians 6:12, or rulers of this age.

These are the highest orders of powers directly under Satan himself, and the ones who clearly were involved in the most critical confrontation of all – engineering the death of Jesus (John 14:30; Luke 22:53; 1 Corinthians 2:6-8).

b. Principalities, princedoms or rulerships (archontes).

These are the powers over territories, perhaps the gods of the nations or the *"sons of God"*, mentioned in Job 1:6 and 38:7.

> *"When the Most High gave to the nations their inheritance, when he separated the sons of men, he fixed the bounds of the peoples according to the number of the sons of God."*
>
> (Deuteronomy 32:8RSV)

These angelic powers originally appointed to watch over the nations have apparently fallen after the fact of Satan's rebellion and have come under his influence (Psalm 82:1-2). They are referred to in Daniel 10:13, 20 as the *"prince of Persia"* and *"the prince of Greece"*.

c. Rulers (archon) Colossians 1:16, Ephesians 1:21, 3:10, 6:12.

These are perhaps the more numerous and lower orders, who are over specific regions, cities or territories.

2. Powers over spheres of influence

Another way of looking at these orders is to see their attachment as being to functional, rather than geographical areas of interest. We can distinguish what seems to be four distinct categories.

a. Dominions or lordships (kuriotes) Colossians 1:16; Ephesians 1:21.
These are demonic officers over particular cultural and social areas of influence. For example political, educational or philosophical ideologies or the media, the legal system or music, entertainment and the arts etc.

b. Powers (dunamis) Romans 8:38; 1 Peter 3:22; Colossians 1:16.
A multiplicity of controlling powers over specific institutions great and small – business corporations, educational establishments, welfare organisations, governing bodies, societies, clubs and associations of all kinds.

c. Authorities (exousia) Colossians 2:15; Ephesians 3:10.
Beings with the right, delegated to them from above, to exercise authority, that is to represent a power source and act on its behalf.

d. Spiritual forces (pneumatikos) of evil in the spiritual realm Ephesians 6:12.
These relate particularly to activity in the realm of spirit such as false prophecy, false religions and heretical doctrine, occultism, witchcraft and the magic arts, and spurious miracles or deceiving signs (Jeremiah 14:14, Ezekiel 13:20-23; Acts 13:6; 1 John 4:1 etc.).

4

Christ and The Powers

In spite of the Fall and the rebellion of mankind, God did not abandon his creation. The Incarnation is, in fact God's ultimate commitment to the work of his hands. The Son of God became part of the created order to redeem it back to its original purpose. The significance of this for the city, that is, the structural principalities and powers is that we must not reject them, abandon them or withdraw from them because –

a. In spite of the fallenness and rebellion of the structural powers, God maintains them in being, otherwise society would fall into chaos (Romans 13:1-6).

b. The demonic powers are the object of divine judgement, but the structural powers are the object of redemption, that is to say, they are not only part of the *"all things"* of creation, in Colossians 1:16-17, they are also part of the *"all things"* of reconciliation in Colossians 1:20.

c. Disarmed of their rebellion, and delivered from demonic control, the structural powers and their gifts are required for the age to come (1 Corinthians 15:24-28; Ephesians 1:10; Revelation 21:24-26).

We now have to see how the disarming and recovery of the powers has been effected.

The powers and first century Palestine

In Galatians 4:4 Paul, referring to the Incarnation, says *"But when the time had fully come, God sent his Son...",* in other words, Jesus came into the world at a uniquely significant time in human history. But when we examine the Palestine of the first century into which we come, we come across a feature that has received very little attention – **He came into a nation that was dominated by the principalities and powers.**

1. The Country was under the heel of a strong military power, the Roman Empire. It was an occupied country, there were foreign troops in complete control of the nation.

2. It was under a legalistic religious power, the synagogue and the Sanhedrin, so intolerant that they tried to assassinate Jesus just because he healed the sick on the Sabbath day.

3. The nation was crushed by the harsh, oppressive, economic and civil power of the Herodians who farmed out the taxes and kept most of the population in abject poverty, to finance their grandiose life style and building projects.

4. More ominous still, the country was under demonic power to an unusual extent. When you read the Old Testament you find very few references to evil spirits and very few examples of demonised people, apart from spirit mediums, astrologers and diviners. But when you turn to the Gospels, they are everywhere, and the casting out of demons was a dramatic part of Jesus' public ministry. The evidence seems to indicate a massive eruption of demons into the nation, as though Satan was expecting an attack on his domain and was preparing against it.

Jesus and the powers

In his Incarnate humanity Jesus lived a life of perfect freedom under the powers. The powers could do nothing with him. None of us are free, the way Jesus was free. We can be managed by one of two traits, one is greed and the other is fear, the carrot or the stick. The powers are confident that every man has his price and every man has his breaking point.

But what do you do with a man like Jesus? He had no greed whatsoever. *"Foxes have holes and birds of the air have nests, but the Son of Man has no place to lay his head"* (Matthew 8:20). Yet he could have had everything he wanted. When the devil offered him the kingdoms of the world in return for his worship, that was nonsense. Jesus could have taken the world over any time he chose, and not by any divine power, but by the sheer moral force of one single perfectly whole and perfectly uncorrupted human will. We have no conception of the moral energy he could have generated had he wanted to. No one could have resisted him. He could have walked into the senate in Rome and said to Caesar, "Get down off that throne. I have taken the world over." But Jesus did not do that, he was after something much greater. He had come to end the sin problem for ever, and that required a Cross.

Furthermore Jesus had no fear. In the boat with the disciples in a demon inspired storm that left them irrational with terror, his response when wakened from sleep was *"Why are you so afraid?"* (Matthew 8:26). What do you do with a man who has no greed and no fear? You can't do anything.

1. Jesus demonstrated his freedom from the power of the synagogue by healing on the Sabbath day. We read that he travelled throughout Galilee, preaching in their synagogues, healing the sick and driving out demons (Matthew 4:23; Mark 1:39). If he did it in the synagogues it would always be on the Sabbath. Why did Jesus deliberately and consistently perform miracles on the Sabbath day? (Matthew 9:35; 12:9-13; Mark 6:1-4; Luke 13:10-16; 14:1-4; John 5:6-10; 9:1-16.) He was refusing to submit to the spirit of the synagogue.

2. Some Pharisees came to Jesus one time and warned him to hide because Herod wanted to kill him. Jesus' reply? *"Go tell that fox, 'I will drive out demons and heal people today and tomorrow, and on the third day I will reach my goal.'"* (Luke 13:32). He refused to submit to the economic/civil power of the house of Herod.

3. When Jesus appears before Pilate, the Roman said, *"Don't you*

realise I have power either to free you or to crucify you?" Jesus' reply showed who was master, *"You would have no power over me if it were not given to you from above"* (John 19:10-11). No wonder it was Pilate who was afraid.

4. Even more dramatically, Jesus faces the strong man, Satan himself (Matthew 4:1-11). There in the most unfavourable of conditions, not in a garden like Eden but in the wilderness, not freshly rested but after 40 days of fasting, he met all the subtlety and power of the fallen archangel, not in one temptation but in three, and came off victorious. Jesus faced Satan, eyeball to eyeball, as the Spirit filled Man, and established once for all his moral ascendancy over the devil. Henceforth in his ministry he drives out the demons with a word; having bound the strong man he proceeds to plunder his house (Matthew 12:25-29).

Jesus taught his disciples the same freedoms – not to be afraid of the power of the synagogue and the ruling authorities (Luke 12:4-11), not to be afraid of the power of possessions and economic survival (Matthew 6:25-35), and not to be afraid of the power of Satan (Luke 10:18-20).

The surrender to the powers

Then at the end of Jesus' three years of ministry we come to the amazing paradox – JESUS SURRENDERS TO THE POWERS. The religious power arrests him without resistance, interrogates him, tries him before the Sanhedrin for blasphemy, and hands him over to the military power. The military power tries to palm the problem off on to the civil power and send him to Herod, then when he is sent back, it brutally flogs him and then crucifies him. The economic power strips him stark naked on the cross and gambles his clothes away.

But there was something even stranger – Jesus surrenders to the satanic power. He said, *"This is your hour, and the power of darkness"* (Luke 22:53RSV). When the sky was darkened as Jesus hung on the Cross, it was not nature hiding its face from the sight, it was the hour and power of darkness. There was one hour in all eternity, one place in the whole universe, when Satan must have thought he had everything in his grasp. He had the Logos, the eternal Son of God, a willing helpless victim in his hands, and he crucified him.

The victory of the Cross

The Cross was Satan's undoing, he never realised until too late what would happen on the Cross, for even in his dying Jesus preserved his freedom, his life was not taken from him, he yielded it up (Luke 23:46).

In 1 Corinthians chapter 2 Paul is dealing with the secret wisdom of God revealed in the Cross, and then he makes this statement:

> *"None of the rulers of this age understood it, for if they had, they would not have crucified the Lord of glory."*
>
> (1 Corinthians 2:8)

The rulers of this age are the demonic world rulers who engineered the death of Jesus. What Paul is saying is that if Satan had had any idea of what was going to happen through the Cross, he would have levelled every tree in Palestine rather than let them use one to crucify Jesus!

What was the wisdom of the Cross?

1. Jesus' death on our behalf, cancelled the destructive power of sin and the punishment of the law that was against us.

> *"When you were dead in your sins and in the uncircumcision of your sinful nature, God made you alive with Christ. He forgave us all our sins, having cancelled the written code, with its regulations, that was against us and that stood opposed to us; he took it away, nailing it to the cross."*
>
> (Colossians 2:13-15)

2. By his death and resurrection Jesus robbed Satan of his

strongest weapon against us, the power of death, and thus effectively disarmed him.

> *"Since the children have flesh and blood, he too shared in their humanity so that by his death he might destroy him who holds the power of death – that is, the devil – and free those who all their lives were held in slavery by their fear of death."* (Hebrews 2:14)

The word destroy is the Greek *katargeo*, literally to reduce to inactivity, thus abolish, disarm, render powerless or nullify.

3. He also disarmed the principalities and powers.

> *"And having disarmed the powers and authorities, he made a public spectacle of them, triumphing over them by the cross."* (Colossians 2:15)

The image here is of the Roman triumph when the defeated foes were led in a public parade behind the victor. In this sense the powers have been exposed, stripped, disarmed and unmasked by the death and resurrection of Jesus.

Which powers have been disarmed?

The question then arises, which powers have been disarmed, the structural powers, represented by the city, or the demonic powers represented by the watching angel behind the city?

The answer is – both! Jesus has established his authority over both the demonic and the structural powers, so that he could say *"All authority in heaven and on earth* (eternal and temporal, spiritual and secular) *has been given to me"* (Matthew 28:18).

The significance of this is momentous.

1. It means that there is authority in the Name of Jesus to enable us to bind the demonic powers in the spiritual realm and cast them

out of the structures, thus opening the structures up to change.

2. It also means that we can challenge the rebelliousness of the structural powers with the claims of the Lordship of Jesus Christ and in the long run they have to yield. That is what makes real cultural change possible.

> *"Jesus Christ, who has gone into heaven and is at God's right hand – with angels, authorities and powers in submission to him."* (1 Peter 3:22)

The source of the victory of the Cross

We still have to ask – what was in the death of Jesus on the Cross that so thoroughly defeated the powers? It was not his death as death that accomplished the victory, nor was it his surrender to the powers. Evil is not overcome by mere surrender to its wickedness as though it will finally be sated by being given a free hand to indulge itself to the utmost.

The power that was in the death of Jesus was that it was death in obedience. *"He became obedient to death – even death on a cross!"* (Philippians 2:8).

What drives the principalities and powers is the energy of rebellion against God. Jesus faced that rebellion with ultimate obedience to the Father's will. All the efforts of the powers was directed to one end, to stir in the human heart of Jesus a flicker of resistance to the Father's will, a flicker of self preservation and resistance to the destiny chosen for him. Their treatment of Jesus can be explained from no other source – the hours of interrogation, the sadistic brutal torture and mockery of a man doomed to die, the taunts to come down from the cross.

But they failed. Jesus met it all with obedience, obedience, obedience, until finally the powers could go no further. His ultimate obedience exhausted the rebellion of the powers until they fell back defeated, debilitated, neutralised and depotentiated. In the end even death had to yield and Jesus rose triumphant over death and Hades.

Now he reigns, and will reign until all the structural powers have been purged of their rebellion and acknowledge his Lordship.

5

Redemption Restores
Creation

In the previous chapter we saw something of the triumph of the Cross over the principalities and powers, both structural and demonic. Now we need to examine what that means for the powers themselves.

God's purpose in redemption was twofold.

1. To restore all creation, with man as its steward, to its original state, under the headship of Christ.

> *"With a view to an administration suitable to the fulness of the times, that is, the summing up of all things in Christ, things in the heavens and things upon the earth."*
>
> (Ephesians 1:10 ASB)

2. Not only to restore creation to its original state but to transform it as the arena for the display of the Father's glory in the age to come.

> *"the creation itself will be liberated from its bondage to decay and brought into the glorious freedom of the children of God."*   (Romans 8:21)

> *"For the earth will be filled with the knowledge of the glory of the Lord, as the waters cover the sea."*   (Habakkuk 2:14)

All the great words of salvation have this common theme of restoring something back to its original state or purpose.

Redemption is bringing back into freedom those who have

gone into slavery.

Regeneration is giving life back to something that has died.

Reconciliation is bringing back into harmony those who are at odds with one another.

Restoration is recovering a former state that has been lost.

Even salvation has the sense of salvaging or bringing back to safety something that is in peril or danger.

How far does redemption reach?

The answer to the question as to how far redemption reaches, is that redemption recovers all that sin has lost. The Blood reaches as far as sin has gone, and sin has ruined, not just mankind, but the whole created order.

> *"We know that the whole creation has been groaning as in the pains of childbirth right up to the present time."*
>
> (Romans 8:22)

The intractable problems of society are not merely the sinfulness of fallen men. There is structural evil, an evil in the systems. All the structures of society, the city, the principalities and powers are also sin-damaged.

But if sin has penetrated the fabric of society, so does the Blood of Christ, "where sin increased, grace increased all the more" (Romans 5:20). The church insists, and rightly so, that salvation is not just a personal matter, it must radically affect my marriage and family relationships. But marriage and family are only one of a whole network of relationships that make up life. Why draw the limit for redemption around the family? Why not my work, my community life or my political affiliation?

There is in fact, no biblical warrant for excluding any of these areas, in fact the reverse. The land is included, and the restoration of the city is included.

> *"If my people, who are called by my name, will humble themselves and pray and seek my face and turn from their*

wicked ways, then will I hear from heaven and will forgive
their sin and will heal their land."   (2 Chronicles 7:14)

Isaiah 61 is the passage that Jesus read out in the synagogue in Nazareth.

"The Spirit of the Lord God is upon me, because the Lord
has anointed me to bring good news to the afflicted; He has
sent me to bind up the brokenhearted, to proclaim liberty to
captives, and freedom to prisoners; to proclaim the
favourable year of the Lord."   (Isaiah 61:1-2 ASB)

Jesus stopped there for his purposes. We go on to apply the next verses to much of what has happened in the charismatic renewal.

"To comfort all who mourn, to grant those who mourn in
Zion, giving them a garland instead of ashes, the oil of
gladness instead of mourning, the mantle of praise instead of
a spirit of fainting. So they will be called oaks of
righteousness, the planting of the Lord, that he may be
glorified."   (Isaiah 61:2-3 ASB)

We stop there, but the prophecy does not stop there, it says *"Then"*, that is after all the foregoing has happened –

"Then they will rebuild the ancient ruins, they will raise up
the former devastations, and they will repair the ruined
cities, the desolations of many generations.
And strangers will stand and pasture your flocks, and
foreigners will be your farmers and your vinedressers. But
you will be called the priests of the Lord; you will be spoken
of as ministers of our God."   (Isaiah 61:4-6 ASB)

The message is clear. When we receive the oil of joy and the mantle of praise we will be called the planting of the Lord.

But when we rebuild the ruined cities, then we will be called the priests of the Lord and the ministers of our God.

Deliverance and Blessing

There are two dominant biblical themes of salvation:

1. Salvation as deliverance. Christ has delivered us from the dominion of darkness (Colossians 1:13 ASB) and from the devil (Hebrews 2:14). God will deliver us from all our troubles (Psalm 34:19), and from all our enemies (Psalm 18:16-19).

2. Salvation as blessing. Christ brings us the blessing of eternal life (Ephesians 2:5), of forgiveness (Colossians 1:14), sanctification (1 Peter 1:2), healing (Acts 10:38), sonship (Galatians 4:5), and inheritance (Ephesians 1:14).

Salvation for the city involves both deliverance and blessing.

1. The demonic principalities over the city have to be overthrown. They are the object of judgement, not the object of redemption. We have to learn, not only how to drive demons out of people, but how to drive demons out of structures, so that the structural powers can be recovered. That is the realm of strategic (level 3), spiritual warfare that we will deal with in chapter 8.

2. The structural powers have to be reclaimed because they are the objects of redemption, not destruction. That will involve:

> *a. Spiritual warfare to quell their rebellion* and unrighteous activities and to overthrow their idolatrous claims.

> *b. Challenging them with the Lordship of Christ* and calling them back to fulfil their rightful destiny as servants of Jesus Christ. This is the realm of redemptive organisational change that we will deal with in chapter 7.

The Final Future of the Powers

Our present response towards the city, and the powers the city symbolises, will depend a great deal on what our perspective is for their future. There is little incentive to spend time and effort on a lost cause.

Thankfully the powers are not a lost cause. Because they are part of the "all things" of creation (Colossians 1:16), their destruction or annihilation in the consummation of all things (Ephesians 1:10) would mark, not a victory for God but a defeat. But they are, as we have seen already, part of the "all things" of reconciliation, and are required for the age to come when we find them subject to the true Head, Jesus Christ, who is seated at God's right hand in the heavenly realm.

> *"far above all rule and authority, power and dominion, and every title that can be given, not only in the present age but also in the one to come."* (Ephesians 1:21)

At present we live in the tension between the Kingdom of God that is both here, and not yet here; present in principle, but not yet present in fullness.

When we examine God's redemptive work in the individual and His redemptive work in the city, we will find that they parallel each other. In each case there are two distinct stages, that can be described as:

　　a. God's continuous work, and
　　b. God's discontinuous work.

1. In the individual

a. God's continuous work is the work of sanctification. In this we are being progressively changed by the Holy Spirit to become in character more and more like Jesus Christ (Romans 8:29; 2 Corinthians 3:18). This will go on all our lives.

b. But when we die, or when Jesus returns, there is God's discontinuous work, the work of glorification. It is a dramatic, instantaneous, radical change that is no more continuance of the work of sanctification. In a moment, in the twinkling of an eye, we will be changed, mortal will be clothed with immortality, the natural body will become a spiritual body of power and glory, and we will be like Jesus because we will see him as he is (1 John 3:2; 1 Corinthians 15:42-44, 52-54; 2 Corinthians 5:4; Philippians 3:21). We can read the words but what they are trying to convey is almost unimaginable.

2. In the principalities and powers

a. God's continuous work in the city is the work of restoration. The city rebels, the city is destroyed, the city repents, like Nineveh (Jonah 3:1-10) and the city is rebuilt, like Jerusalem (Nehemiah 2:5-6:15).

b. God's discontinuous work, is the work of transformation. In the end the transformed city, the New Jerusalem comes down from God out of heaven (Revelation 21:2-27). It is a city of unimaginable beauty and splendour, and –

> *"The nations will walk by its light, and the kings of the earth will bring their splendour into it. On no day will its gates ever be shut, for there will be no night there. The glory and honour of the nations will be brought into it."*

> (Revelation 21:24-26)

What is to be our present response?

Here we tend to come up against competing eschatologies. One scenario says in effect that the powers (the city) is either beyond redemption or is merely to be testified against, or its recovery is none of our business because Christ is going to do it all at his Second Coming. That would be like saying that our ongoing struggle against personal sin and failure is hopeless, or it is unnecessary because we are all going to be perfect anyway when Jesus comes. No-one could find warrant for that view in Scripture.

The other scenario says that it is our responsibility to christianise the whole world and the whole institutional structure of society before it is possible for Jesus to come back and reign.

That is like saying we will gradually become more and more holy and more and more perfect until one day we are too good for this earth and Jesus will have to take us into heaven.

The truth lies between these extremes.

It is evident from Scripture and experience that it is possible, before Jesus comes back, to have redeemed individuals who are not yet perfect, but who are radically changed from what they were before.

In the same way, it is possible, before Jesus returns, to have redeemed but not perfect business organisations, redeemed but not perfect economic systems and educational institutions, redeemed but not perfect cities and redeemed but not perfect nations.

It is to the practical implications of these truths that we now turn.

6

Living with Principalities and Powers

How then, as Christians, are we meant to live amongst the structural powers? For live in them we must in one manifestation or other. A useful way to approach the question is to go back to the three levels mentioned in chapter 1:

Level I The individual or personal level
Level II The suprahuman or structural level
Level III The supernatural or demonic level

The Individual and the Powers

This is the most common level at which we experience the reality of the principalities and powers. We meet them in businesses, at school, in hospitals or government offices, in clubs and in the local church. We are involved with them in every area of our life. Here are the important points to remember.

1. Regardless of the fallenness of the powers we can live and work in them and, like Daniel or Joseph, serve their legitimate ends and rise to positions of authority and influence in them. In doing so, moreover, we are to serve wholeheartedly, as if we are serving the Lord, not men (Ephesians 6:5-7) and we are to give everyone their due, whether it is taxes, or payment or respect or honour (Romans 13:7).

2. But while we live in the powers and serve their ends, we also live under the Lordship of Christ and that guarantees our moral freedom. Therefore we are not to yield to the idolatrous spirit of the powers, but to walk in faith and obedience like Shadrach, Meshach and Abednego (Daniel 3:1ff) and like Daniel himself (Daniel 6:1ff). That means:

a. We are not to take our moral standards or our value system from the principalities and powers, or allow them to water down our Christian values so that they conform to the mind-set of the world. Read again the biblical character analysis of the city (chapter 2) and you will see why we need to have our minds continually renewed by the Holy Spirit and the word of God (Romans 12:2).

b. We must never allow the powers to become the ultimate authority in our lives as they will always try to do. In fact if you yield to the spirit of an organisation, you can break all its rules and it will still look after you. If you refuse to yield to the corporate spirit, you may keep all its rules but it will try to get rid of you or try to destroy you. Only our willing submission to the Lordship of Christ guarantees our freedom against the powers. If we bow to Christ we need not bow to Caesar.

c. We must reckon realistically with the fact that from time to time we will also come under spiritual attack from demonic principalities and powers. Remember that the attack will most often come through people, but people are never the enemy. It often takes real discernment to identify the true source of the attack (Matthew 16:21-23). Furthermore, we need to understand the principles of defensive warfare so that we can maintain our ground.

Defensive Spiritual Warfare

The situations in which we are likely to come under spiritual attack from demonic principalities and powers could be one of the following:

1. We are threatening the enemy's possessions or position. Even a lone Christian standing simply in the Lordship of Jesus is posing an awesome threat to the fancied omnipotence of the powers, both structural and demonic.

2. The enemy is probing for our weaknesses, because Satan believes that we all have our price and our areas of vulnerability.

3. The enemy is trying to disable our defences, isolate us from God and from other believers, and if possible seduce us or destroy us.

The principles of defensive warfare

Here are the main principles we must master to overcome in situations where the enemy is attacking us.

1. Occupy the high ground

The high ground is the ground where we have access to power, knowledge and defensive resources. Notice David's reliance on the spiritual high ground of God's presence (Psalm 18:2-3; 16-19; 27:5; 61:2-3 etc.). Our high ground is:

> *a. Our revelation standing or position in Christ.*
> *"God raised us up with Christ and seated us with him in the heavenly realms in Christ Jesus"* (Ephesians 2:6. See also Ephesians 1:18-23; Colossians 3:1-4).

> *b. The victory of the cross and resurrection of Christ.*
> In the New Testament sometimes summarised as *"the blood of the Lamb"* (Colossians 2:15; Hebrews 2:14; Revelation 12:11).

> *c. Our position in the body of Christ and in the covenantal relationships belonging to it* (Ephesians 4:10-16).

Satan will always try to draw us off our high ground and on to his ground by deception or by capitalising on areas of ignorance, or by tempting us to rebellion.

2. Build an effective defence system

This is all-important. Our defence system must be in place before it is needed and must become familiar to us and effective through practice. Note the following important aspects.

a. *Develop an attitude of confidence* (Psalm 27:3; Jeremiah 17:7)

Deal with fear. Fear destroys morale (Deuteronomy 20:8) and tends to produce the very thing we are afraid of (Job 3:25). The answer to fear is, like Elisha's servant, to see the true reality of the situation we face – *"Those who are with us are more than those who are with them,"* (2 Kings 6:15-17) or like Paul – *"If God is for us, who can be against us?"* (Romans 8:31).

b. *Clear away entanglements* that inhibit our effectiveness and render us vulnerable.

These may include relational entanglements (2 Corinthians 6:14), financial entanglements (1 Timothy 6:9-10), debilitating habits or thought patterns that drain our energy (Matthew 6:25-34; 1 Corinthians 9:25-27), non-productive activities that merely complicate things and issues, or circumstances that are not really our responsibility (Hebrews 12:1).

c. *Understand the importance of the armour of God.*

The armour of God is a set of life conditions that God wants to establish in our lives, that enable him to work and prevent Satan from working. But we have to "put on" the armour, that is to say, life conditions only work if we make them ours; they cannot be imposed on us or imparted to us without our deliberate appropriation.

There are many life conditions that are important in our Christian life but it seems that the following ones are vital in terms of spiritual warfare:

i. *Truth* (Ephesians 6:14; 2 Corinthians 6:7). The effect of truth is to expose untruth and therefore protect us from the devil's lies and deception (John 3:19-20).

ii. *Righteousness.* Our covenant relationship with God through Christ, that guarantees our safety and ensures victory (Ephesians 6:14; 2 Corinthians 6:7; Isaiah 59:17).

iii. *Peace* (Ephesians 6:15; Romans 16:20). Not only peace with God but the peace of God to guard or garrison our hearts and minds (Philippians 4:7; Colossians 3:15).

iv. *Faith* (Ephesians 6:16; 1 Thessalonians 5:8). Faith is the creative link that enables God's power to be shared with man (1 John 5:4).

v. *Hope* (Ephesians 6:17; 1 Thessalonians 5:8). Hope is the confident expectation of something good, in other words the openness that enables us to receive.

vi. *Love* (1 Thessalonians 5:8; 2 Corinthians 6:6). That not only links us to the life of God, but is the life of God and overcomes the world (1 John 5:2-5).

vii. *The word of God* (Ephesians 6:17). This is the rhema, the Spirit quickened revelatory word with which Jesus overcame Satan, with which he sustains all things in being (Hebrews 1:3). It is of eternal relevance and effectiveness, *"the word* (rhema) *of the Lord stands forever"* (1 Peter 1:25).

vii. *Prayer in the Spirit* (Ephesians 6:18; Jude 20). Important for building up or strengthening the human spirit.

d. *Examine your resources*

Assess your personal life and experience to discover:

i. *Your spiritual strengths,* the things you know and the things you do well. These are things you need to build on.

ii. *Your weaknesses and vulnerabilities*. These are things for which you may need to devise protective strategies.

iii. *Your relationships*, those people you can depend on for support in difficult times and with whom you can work effectively.

e. Learn to handle spiritual pressure
Under pressure or attack we revert to our deepest responses – the things we truly know and the things we can trust in any and every circumstance. But spiritual attack or pressure rarely sends any advance warning so we need to know:

i. The nature of the truth that constitutes our secure ground.

ii. How to fall back instinctively and automatically on to that strong place, so that it is a well practised manoeuvre.

3. Learn from the experiences

We want to do more than just survive attacks or successfully defend our position. We can learn useful lessons from them if we pay attention.

a. We can discover our weaknesses that cause us to sin and experience grace to overcome next time.

b. We can find out Satan's views as to where our vulnerabilities lie and can develop protective strategies to counter such attacks.

c. We can experience God's interventions on our behalf and build our faith and confidence for the future (2 Corinthian 1:10).

d. We can learn the spiritual skills of interdependence within the Body of Christ, where we stand together against the enemy (Ephesians 6:19).

7

Redeeming the
Structural Powers

Living and working in the powers but keeping ourselves free from their pressure to conform is important, but even more important is recovering them to their rightful role as servants of Jesus Christ the Lord. That is rebuilding the ruined cities.

Remember always that we are dealing with two different dimensions of the problem:

1. Spiritual warfare against the demonic powers behind the structures. The structural powers will resist change in any event, but the demonic powers will, unless they are dealt with, reinforce that resistance, and wear out those who attempt to alter the status quo.

2. Influence and redemptive organisational change in the structural powers. *The two must go hand in hand for if we do not become actively engaged in working for organisational change, all our spiritual warfare will be unproductive, or even counter productive as Jesus warned in Matthew 12:43-45.* What is usually overlooked in this passage is that Jesus applied the analogy of the re-demonised individual to describe the state of an entire society.

Identifying the Character of the Powers

Our first task is to identify the corporate culture or inner spirit of the city, so that we understand that character of the power we are seeking to influence. That involves observation and inquiry, specifically into the following areas.

1. The physical environment

The state of buildings, facilities and the physical surroundings says a good deal about the character of the power, just as the state of a house tells you a lot about the occupants. For example, are they dirty neglected and run-down, or bright, clean and modern; a stark, sterile, concrete jungle; a makeshift, secondhand jumble, or a tasteful, conservative, decor?

2. What the city says about itself

This is the self image of the city. It can be discovered from:

a. Reports, press releases, advertisements and pronouncements by public officials, etc.
b. Its origins and recorded history.
c. More important, the unofficial history and its popular myths, anecdotes and legends.

3. How it greets strangers

a. How the "in" group is distinguished from the "out" group.
b. How those "inside" talk about or treat "outsiders". Are they welcomed or ignored, appreciated or resented, treated as visitors or intruders, looked up to or looked down on, etc.?

4. The shared values

Shared values are the basic concepts and beliefs widely held and endorsed by the organisation. These may not be at all what they are officially said to be, but they can be inferred from:

a. The activities people spend most of their time and energy on.
b. The things that are regarded as the keys to success or acceptance.
c. The things that get the most public attention – media publicity, advertising budgets etc.
d. The things that people talk about most or that create the

greatest controversy – opinion pools, talk back shows, letters to the press etc.

e. The things that draw the biggest crowds.

5. *The Heroes*

Heroes are individuals who personify the shared values of the culture. They are found amongst:

a. Those who are prominent in the public eye as making success seem attainable.

b. Those who provide role-models for others to follow, emulate or aspire to be like.

c. Those who set the fashions in dress, behaviour or lifestyle.

d. Historical figures and the stories, myths and legends that accumulate around them.

6. *The Rituals*

Rituals are expressive events that help to underscore and communicate the shared values of the culture, for example:

a. Social rituals that show how to get into the culture, or what social standards are acceptable in it.

b. Recognition rituals, that is, how success or achievement is recognised or rewarded.

c. Extravaganzas, such as celebrations, commemorations or festivals.

Organisational Change Agent – Nehemiah

A detailed biblical blueprint for organisational change can be found in the book of Nehemiah. It has particular relevance to our present study because it deals with the rebuilding of the city. The temple had been rebuilt by Ezra 70 years before but the city was still in ruins. The last 30 years of the charismatic renewal has seen a substantial rebuilding of the church, but our society, the city, is in ruins.

Here is a summary of Nehemiah's method. It has widespread application to the 'cities' in which we live and work today.

1. Care for the city

When Nehemiah heard of the state of Jerusalem he *"sat down and wept and mourned for days"* (Nehemiah 1:4 ASB). John Greenleaf says that the problem with our society is that nobody loves the institutions. We fear and dislike the structural powers, we are overawed and repelled by them, we submit to them and are sometimes bought and seduced by them, but we do not care for them. Care is nothing less than love in action and if we are ever going to change the city we need to care for it the way a Jew cared for Jerusalem.

> *"If I forget you, O Jerusalem,*
> *may my right hand forget its skill.*
> *May my tongue cling to the roof of my mouth*
> *if I do not remember you,*
> *if I do not consider Jerusalem my highest joy."*

(Psalm 137:5-6)

2. Pray for the city

"For some days I mourned and fasted and prayed before the God of Heaven..." (Nehemiah 1:4-11). Nehemiah's prayer contains two valuable insights for organisational change agents.

a. He identified himself with the sin of the city. *"confess the sins we Israelites, including myself and my father's house, have committed against you'* (Nehemiah 1:6). The city is a corporate entity with corporate evil and because we are a part of its corporate existence we share a real corporate responsibility for its wrongdoing.

b. He was willing to become part of the answer to his own prayer (Nehemiah 1:11). Genuine intercession very often leads to intervention but genuine intercession also requires of the intercessor the willingness to be the one who undertakes the intervention.

3. Plan for the city

A period of about four months elapsed between the events of chapter 1 and those of chapter 2 of Nehemiah when Nehemiah appeared before the king and queen. What he asked for then was not the result of instant inspiration but the fruit of weeks of prayer and careful deliberation. What came out of that preparation was,

a. A big vision
What 50,000 Jews under Zerubbabel had failed to accomplish in 70 years, Nehemiah decided he would do. He said *"I can rebuild it."* (ch.2:5). When it comes to changing a power or rebuilding a city, great or small, we will accomplish nothing without a vision that is big enough to go for radical and not mere cosmetic change.

b. A long term goal
The king asked Nehemiah how long he would be away and Nehemiah *"set a time"* (ch.2:6). Compare chapter 2:1 and chapter 12:6 and you find the time was 12 years! Institutional change takes time and the more radical the changes the longer it will take, therefore to succeed we have to be committed for the long haul.

4. Live in the city

With a true instinct for what was involved Nehemiah came and lived in the city (ch.2:11). We will never change an institution unless we get "in" because change can only come from within. Getting in will require a respectful, non-judgemental and humble willingness to learn the ways of the city and share in its life.

5. Know the city

By the time Nehemiah had been in the city for less than a week he knew its state and its problems as well as anyone:

a. He saw its problems with the objectivity and fresh eyes of a newcomer not conditioned by the culture to accept its ways.

b. He examined the situation personally and at first hand so he could make up his mind without the excuses and rationalisations of the inhabitants, and most important of all;

c. He saw the problems from the perspective of someone who believed they could be overcome and who intended to do something about it.

6. Start a movement

Radical change in a culture or the life of an organisation is always accomplished by a "movement" which has the specific aim of bringing about the desired changes. A movement does not require a majority before it can be launched. It can be initiated by a small dedicated minority, but once launched it can gain a momentum of its own. What Nehemiah did was to initiate just such a movement. Here is his strategy which can be applied to small and large scale organisations alike.

a. Find the influencers, (ch.2:16) the key people whose views count and who set the trends other people follow.

b. Get them to face the problem (ch.2:17), but note that Nehemiah made their problem his too. He said "You see the trouble we are in." He did not say "See the trouble you are in." The identification of the change agent with the problem is all important.

c. Give them a vision (ch.2:17). *"Come let us rebuild the walls of Jerusalem and we will no longer be in disgrace."* But note that Nehemiah was not just talking vision, he had already made some of the critical decisions that would make it possible to actualise the vision (ch.2:7, 18).

d. Get them to buy into the vision for themselves "Then they replied 'Let us start rebuilding'" (ch.2:18). This is the critical point in any movement for change, it has to be owned by those who will run with it, so that it is no longer the vision of the change agent, it is the vision of the movement.

7. Foster the growth of the movement for change

These are the characteristics that need to be identified and then fostered or encouraged.

a. Personal commitment by individuals who believe they can change their immediate environment.
b. Recruitment of friends and colleagues to join in small scale efforts, or "winnable opportunities" for change. The successful movements accumulate a track record of small but observable success in changing things until gradually they accumulate growing support (see ch.3).
c. Expectation of, and willingness to face opposition from the establishment. When a movement is under way, opposition and attack only strengthens its resolve (ch.2:20, 4:1ff).
d. The willingness to go for radical and fundamental rather than peripheral change and the ability to discern the difference. Nehemiah faced the threat of violent opposition but also the more subtle distraction of a negotiated settlement (ch.6:1-9).

8. Reiterate, reinforce and restate the goals as required along the way

Even when change is under way the work is not finished:
a. The vision has to be repeated and expressed in ways that are appropriate to each stage of the movement's development.
b. People have to be continually encouraged, motivated, corrected and sometimes disciplined along the way (ch.4:14, 5:1-13).
c. Difficulties have to be faced, problems solved and the movement represented to the outside world (ch.4:16-20).

9. Finally, along with and even after radical change, there is the on-going process of re-educating and re-ordering the inner life of the city.

The first 6 chapters of Nehemiah deal with the rebuilding of the walls of the city, the next 6 chapters deal with the even more difficult task of reforming its character. The last chapter is a timely warning that the task is never complete in this age, and the possibility of backsliding into the old ways is an ever present possibility.

8

Strategic Level
Spiritual Warfare

Dealing with the Strong Man

We come now to probably the most serious level of the conflict: strategic level spiritual warfare against demonic principalities and powers that dominate and manipulate the structural powers. Their influence is seen at all levels and just as readily in boardrooms and council chambers, with the confusing of ethical issues, the blatant amorality of some decisions and the overall sense of something vastly wise operating behind the scenes and manipulating the puppets.

Dealing with these powers is a matter of first order of importance otherwise our efforts to recover the structural powers for the Kingdom are doomed to failure. Jesus emphasised this when he said,

> *"Or how can anyone enter the strong man's house and carry off his property, unless he first binds the strong man? Then he will plunder his goods."* (Matthew 12:29 ASB)

While Satan is **the** strong man, there will generally be in any specific territory or functional area in which an organisation operates, a *"strong man"* who represents the power source and the dominating influence in that particular area. To attempt to change the attitude and culture of a city or a single organisation before the demonic powers are dealt with, is like trying to rob a strong man's house while the strong man is still there and unhampered in his activity.

> *"When a strong man, fully armed, guards his own house, his possessions are safe. But when someone stronger attacks*

*him and overpowers him, he takes away the armour in which
the man trusted and divides up the spoils." (Luke 11:21, 22)*

This is the realm of offensive spiritual warfare. It is not the place for rash, impetuous and ill conceived forays by enthusiastic raw recruits and needs to be treated with the seriousness with which it is dealt in Scripture.

Offensive Spiritual Warfare

It must be emphasised again that what we are dealing with is neither imaginary or metaphorical war, it is real spiritual war with real enemies, real spiritual bullets and sadly, real casualties. At the same time our objective is always total victory, and the complete confusion and defeat of the enemy (Exodus 17:13-14). Defeat is a shame and dishonour (2 Kings 19:3), there are no points for a "good show" or a good loser.

It is also important to understand that spiritual warfare is necessary for our full development. ***Thus we should not be
surprised to discover that to Israel, peace (shalom) did not mean
the absence of war, it meant:***
a. Complete harmony and unity among friends, and
b. Complete victory in the war against enemies.

That is why Paul could write to the Romans *"The God of peace
will soon crush Satan under your feet"* (Romans 16:20).

Principles of Offensive Warfare

The dynamics of war in the spirit realm are exactly the same as war in the material realm, therefore the Bible is our battle manual and we can cease making apologies for the wars of Israel that are recorded there. In terms of spiritual warfare they take on a dramatic contemporary significance. Here are some of the important aspects that we need to take into account.

We need to prepare for battle

1. All war, including spiritual warfare is a corporate endeavour, in which the army represents the strength of the whole people, in condensed, intensified form. Therefore numbers are not important to success, but unity is (Judges 7:1-7).

2. *Our personal preparedness is vital in terms of both commitment and personal holiness* if we are going to overcome in a spiritual battle with the forces of evil. We need to reckon with the fact that the enemy knows us and knows our weaknesses very well.

a. In Israel, the warrior's state was known as *"kodesh"*, or the state of holiness, that is, the soldiers were separated to their task. In the life of the soldier, war takes priority over all civilian affairs (2 Timothy 2:4).

b. For the army to have the concentrated strength that was needed for battle, every man in it had to possess absolute purity, because impurity destroys the integrity and strength of the soul. Purity is endangered by such things as:
i. Physical, sexual or religious uncleanness (Deuteronomy 23:10-15; Numbers 5:1-4; 1 Samuel 21:6).
ii. Fear. The fearful were sent home because fear destroys morale (Deuteronomy 20:8; Judges 7:3).
iii Unfinished projects, because they could endanger a man's separation or singleness of heart (Deuteronomy 20:5-7).

3. *Spiritual warfare is a conflict of spiritual power, therefore our relationship with God is all important* and it is in the place of prayer and worship that the victory is obtained.
To Israel also, spiritual power alone decided the outcome in battle. *"No king is saved by the size of his army."* (Psalm 33:16). Therefore for the army to have power, its relationship with God must be right. Thus war is ushered in by:

a. *The blowing of the silver trumpets* (Numbers 10:9) so that *"you will be remembered by the Lord your God and rescued from your enemies."* Silver means redemption, because the basis of our victory is the Cross.

b. The sacrifice of the burnt offering that signified worship and thanksgiving. In one sense the whole purpose of our spiritual warfare is the restoration of worship, thus reversing Satan's rebellion and reasserting God's rightful place as Creator and man's rightful place as worshipping creature. *But victory for Israel also begins in the sanctuary, because it is there that strength is received.*

> *"May the Lord answer you when you are in distress; may the name of the God of Jacob protect you.*
> *May he send you help from the sanctuary and grant you support from Zion.*
> *May he remember all your sacrifices and accept your burnt offerings. Selah*
> *May he give you the desire of your heart and make all your plans succeed.*
> *We will shout for joy when you are victorious and will lift up our banners in the name of our God."* (Psalm 20:1-5)

The Nature of Warfare

The following principles are of critical importance for us to understand the real issues of spiritual warfare, and the means to victory.

1. To Israel, the outcome of the war depends entirely on the kings. The war is his war and, because it is spiritual power that decides the issue, victory depends on the king having victory in his soul. *His soul must be filled with victory before the battle, because the actual outcome of the battle is only the manifestation of the real victory or defeat that already exists* (Psalm 18:32-34; 1 Kings 20:13ff; 22:1ff).

Our final victory in the spiritual warfare with Satan and his hosts is absolutely assured because *Jesus Christ, our King has total victory in his soul. "He must reign until he has put all his enemies under his feet"* (1 Corinthians 15:25; Psalm 110:1-2). Real victory already exists and the outcome of any battle is only the outward manifestation of what is already in Christ's soul.

2. The decisive spiritual thing in war is for the king to have what is called "strong counsel", that is, irresistible thoughts that are immediately carried out.

a. By counsel is meant not just advice or suggestion, but the fullest expression of the king's mind and will, his plans, strategies, purposes, resolve and assurance.

b. God is *"great in counsel and mighty in deed"* (Jeremiah 32:19) therefore his word carries in itself the power to accomplish what it declares, therefore,

i. God's counsel, that is his plans and purposes always succeed.

> *"The Lord Almighty has sworn, 'Surely as I have planned, so it will be, and as I have purposed, so it will stand.'"*
> (Isaiah 14:24)

ii. God breaks and shatters all counsel or plans directed against him and against his people.

> *"Prepare for battle and be shattered! Prepare for battle and be shattered! Devise your strategy, but it will be thwarted; propose your plan but it will not stand, for God is with us."*
> (Isaiah 8:9-10)

iii. God's counsel confuses and dissolves the enemy's counsel so that it cannot take effect. Thereby, the morale of the enemy is destroyed and his will weakened and paralysed (Jeremiah 50:35-38; Isaiah 19:1-4).

3. The king's counsel penetrates the heart of his people and bends their will to his so that they become one soul. The victory in the king's soul becomes the victory in their soul. (Revelation 12:11; John 16:33). The victory that is in Christ must penetrate our heart and soul so that his victory also becomes ours (1 John 4:4; 5:4).

"I saw Satan fall like lightning from heaven. I have given you authority to trample on snakes and scorpions and to overcome all the power of the enemy; nothing will harm you." Luke 10:18-19

4. Note the importance of the prophetic ministry. In Israel, the prophet played a great part in creating victory in the king's soul, because they were able to "see" whether it was there. If they could see victory or defeat it was settled as a reality! (Kings 22:1-40).

The critical issue in our warfare is whether we have in our soul the victory that is in Christ's soul. That is a matter of revelation. The function of the prophetic ministry is to give us the strong counsel based on revelation that will actualise that victory in us also.

The Conduct of the Battle

1. Remember that God directs the campaign and determines the strategy. That strategy will vary from place to place and from time to time (Joshua 5:13-15, 6:5, 8:1; Numbers 21:34, 30:1ff; 1 Samuel 7:10, 23:2, 30:7).

2. Remember you do not have the whole front to take care of, all you have is a limited, local objective.
a. If you do not take that objective, nobody else will do it for you.
b. You have to do it whether you think you can or not and whether you are afraid or not.

3. Learn to use the prophetic word of Scripture as it is quickened to you by the Holy Spirit in,
a. Speaking the judgement word of God into being against the demonic powers, or
b. Holding the commands of God with your will against the will of the powers, or
c. Declaring to the powers the greatness and majesty, the power

and holiness, the victory and the coming again of Jesus Christ, in order to weaken and terrify them.

4. *Learn to discern the critical issues of timing in warfare.*
a. Watching for God's hand, "seeing" what the Father is doing (John 5:19).
b. Discerning the enemy's weakness or attention lapses and capitalising on them; seizing the momentum of a battle (2 Kings 13:14-20).
c. Waiting for the proceeding word of God that says "Go" (1 Samuel 23:2-4).

5. *Understand the law of occupation.* If you take a territory you must have the resources to hold it and to occupy it, *"lest the wild beasts multiply"* (Deuteronomy 7:22).

Abijah and Jereboam

An illustration of many of the principles of warfare that we have been discussing will be found in the account of the battle between Abijah, king of Judah and Jereboam, king of Israel in 2 Chronicles 13:1-20.

1. Abijah was on the defensive, because Jereboam had superiority in numbers by 2 to 1 (v5) and tactical superiority; he had Abijah's army ambushed front and rear (v13).

2. Victory depended on the persons of the two kings. Abijah occupies the high ground (v4) and endeavours both to plant victory in his own soul and to plant defeat in Jereboam's soul (vv4-12).

3. He does this by also occupying the spiritual high ground, rehearsing the rights of Judah as the kingdom of the Lord and the Davidic dynasty (v8) the nation's faithfulness to the true priesthood and the true worship of God (vv 10-11). He contrasts it with Jereboam's kingdom, born in rebellion and nurtured in idolatry.

4. When Judah found themselves under attack front and rear, they cried out to the Lord, the priests blew the silver trumpets, the warriors shouted the faith statement of the battle cry *"The Lord has given our enemies into our hands"* and Israel fled before Judah (vv 14-16).

5. Finally Abijah pursued Jereboam to complete and humiliating defeat so that Jereboam never regained his power again during Abijah's reign.